The Majesty of An *Eagle*

The Majesty of An *Eagle*

Your Attitude Determines the Altitude of Your Flight

Dr M A Monareng

ISBN:	Softcover	978-1-4797-2114-6
	Ebook	978-1-4797-2115-3

This book was printed in the United States of America.

To order additional copies of this book, contact:
Xlibris Corporation
0-800-644-6988
www.xlibrispublishing.co.uk
Orders@xlibrispublishing.co.uk
303903

Dedication

I wish to dedicate this book to my parents Taziana and Bareng who have already been called to higher service. During the early years of my life they believed and instilled self-confidence in me. To my wife Annah and my three sons Thabo, Tshepo and Thato who are always a source of encouragement. They are indeed a blessing from above.

Contents

CHAPTER 1

The Power of Integrity

By definition, integrity is a state of completeness and wholeness, strict adherence to a code of moral rules. People of integrity are respected for their quality of being honest and firm in their moral principles.

A man of the highest integrity means what he says, says what he means and does what he means. Integrity is a commitment to be aware of our behaviour, and accept responsibility for our actions, take corrective measures when we are out of line with our moral codes to bring ourselves back into a desired state of life.

When one takes a stand for something, then by default, other people know what that person is against. People of integrity stand for certain values. These values are the ground motives of their lives. Integrity should therefore be a way of life for teachers, spiritual leaders, political leaders, families and all the other people. Our biggest problem is the fact that the headlines of our national newspapers are dominated by the disgraceful conducts of our leaders.

Great teachers know that if they can become professionally more unique than their colleagues, they will be remembered more easily and more often by their students. Their unique identity can be accomplished through their way of speaking, clothing and personal conduct.

We have seen too many examples of leaders in our country and the world at large, who lack integrity. Leaders need to be aware of the fact that people need a leader with integrity. Leaders who want to be respected by people. Leaders who should be leading an exemplary life style worth emulating.

In the working environment in any organisation, employees want to work under a leader or manager who has integrity. In the absence of integrity, employees will miss a vital ingredient in their ability to perform their duties. Leaders with integrity make it safe for their subordinates to perform at their peak. Such a leader knows that there is safety in providing freedom for people to create openness and honesty among them.

This consistent character incumbent on great leaders is integrity. How much do we value integrity?

King Solomon who was known for his wisdom, his wealth and his writings valued integrity **(Proverbs 10:9) "People with integrity walk safely, but those who follow crooked paths will slip and fall".**

Integrity is about keeping our promises and doing what we said we would definitely do. We cannot lead the lives of half truth, empty promises and half commitment. When you are to join your friend to travel together, and you are late, and are about fifty kilometres away, but you call to say that you are ten kilometres away, are you really a person of integrity? This might seem like an insignificant matter, but for a person of integrity, this is a very important issue. If we do not walk in integrity we are not only faking honesty but cheating ourselves. Everyone has a book to write in this world. Through one's walks, talks and actions people can read chapter by chapter in our lives.

Integrity is therefore important in helping us to make right adjustments and take responsibility in doing what is correct.

A true leader must walk his talk, but in order to uphold the credibility of his talk, the leader has to live it himself. When his behaviour is exemplary by being true to his talk, there is authenticity and credibility and his followers sense integrity. Where there is integrity there is trust. In the presence of trust there are committed followers. Where there are committed followers great leadership can be noticed.

I read broadly about animals and birds and watched many of them as a herdsboy. These creatures have a special place in the lives of many Africans. African surnames are directly or indirectly named after some birds or animals. Proverbs and idiomatic expressions have been composed about them.

Africans respect birds and animals as they give special messages about seasons of the year and some give a warning to people when danger is rearing its ugly head and are unaware of it.

Of all these creatures, the most fascinating for me is an eagle. Because of their strength, eagles have been a symbol of war and imperial power since the Babylonian times. Eagles from birth have very unique innate and physical characteristics. They are born with their mouths open and their eyes looking into the sun.

This skilful hunting bird is regarded as the nobility of the feathered society, from the plains of Africa and rivers of Alaska to the forests of the Philippines and the seas of Japan

The eagle is the most majestic of all birds and is mentioned ***not less than twenty-five times in the Bible*** much more than other birds. This is the bird of integrity which can in most cases serve as a role model far much better than the human race which is the crown of creation.

Eagles, for centuries have fascinated and inspired many people especially Christians. Eagle eyes are too keen for them to can blindly fly into danger.

Studies suggest that some eagles can spot an animal the size of a rabbit up to three kilometres away. These are the masters of the sky. They are venerated as living symbols of power, freedom, and transcendence. Some religions believe that high-soaring eagles are capable of touching the face of God. The eagle is distinguished from the vulture as it is used on occasion to symbolise the God's people. There are four creatures symbolising the four Evangelists in the four synoptic gospels.

Matthew the Evangelist, is symbolised by a man or angel ; Mark the Evangelist is symbolised by a lion ; Luke the Evangelist is symbolised by an ox or bull and finally, John the Evangelist, is symbolised by an eagle, a figure of the sky believed to be able to look straight into the sun. It represents Jesus' Ascension, and Christ's divine nature.

Of all the birds of th e wild, it is the eagle which is so highly regarded that it is described at a higher level than the other three.

It is highly valued due to its majesty and power of integrity.

An Eagle logo is a National Symbol of the US, it was a symbol of Hitler, Napoleon and Julius Caesar. All of them did not use any other animal but the Eagle as it has always been the symbol of leadership and power.

Eagles do not fly, they soar

Eagles were created to be free and to soar to great heights. Man as a crown of creation has been created to remain pure and holy and conform to His image. Eagles do not fly like other birds by flapping their wings but rather soar. Flapping their wings would cause them to use an credible amounts of their own strength and endurance and that would require much more energy to do so. Instead they sit on a high ledge and wait for the storm to come. Mind you an eagle knows instinctively when a storm is approaching long before it breaks.

The eagle will fly to some high spot and wait for the winds to come. When the storm hits, it sets its wings so that the wind will pick it up and lift it above the storm. While the storm rages below, the eagle is soaring above it.

The eagle has used the right time, it takes off and soars upward, effortlessly, because it has waited for the right time. There is a special wind currents, that they ride as it circles higher and higher toward the sky.

What makes the eagle special is that she sits on the rock and reads the wind and when the time is perfect she takes off and soars upward effortlessly with her great wings. She just spreads her wings and rides the wind and circle higher and higher into the sky.

Most often man act impulsively, jumping out too soon, causing a lot of disorder and chaos and missing a point by failing to wait for God's perfect timing.

God is a God of time. He knows His time, He knows your time and He knows my time. We are living in the days of speed , during the time when the concept Waiting is foreign to both the believers and non-believers. But when we wait on the Lord—wait for His timing—wait for His answers—wait for His direction then we can soar to new heights and fly to new places. Isaiah 40:28-31: "**Those who wait on the Lord will renew their strength, they will soar on wings like eagles: they will run and not grow weary, they will walk and not faint.**" If you patiently wait for the presence of the Lord, your weakness will be exchanged for His strength. He knows the future, He knows tomorrow, He knows the way , **He is the way (John 14:6.)**

A person of integrity cannot be out of touch with God's will for very long.

The integrity of the upright shall guide them: but the perverseness of transgressors shall destroy them (Proverb 11: 3).

Integrity will guide you. It will preserve, promote and protect you. A person of integrity is sincere. You can take that person's word at face value. You may not speak in tongues, be able to give a moving testimony or lay hands on the sick and see them recover, but you can be honest. Integrity is a product of heart character. It is very powerful. Integrity will establish you, and finally it will please God if you are a person of integrity.

CHAPTER 2

The power of Attitude and Choice

Attitude and choice are everything in the life of every person.

Choice determines things you wish to do in life, but how well you do those things depends on your attitude. If you allow your circumstances to control your attitude, you will not be able to accomplish anything positive in life. Everyone has a power to choose the attitude he or she will embrace for the day in any situation. J. Martin Kohe says **"the greatest power that a person possesses is the power to choose".**

Yes we are living in the world of choices and life is about the choice we make. And how successful or unsuccessful you are today and you will be tomorrow, is determined by the choice of your attitude. You are at the driver's seat of your own life.

The difference between the eagle and the pigeon when the storm approaches, it's their attitudes. Their attitude and reaction towards the storm determines their survival.

You have got the POWER to choose.

- You have the power to choose the political home or party you like.
- You have the power to choose friends—the kind of friends who will help you succeed in achieving your goals or friends that will contribute towards the destruction of your future.

- You have the power to choose today what you want to be tomorrow; to choose the career that will bring happiness in your life or the career that will bring you frustrations throughout your life.

- You have the power to choose your future partner—the partner that will bring you paramount conviviality or melancholy in your life.

- You have the power to choose your lifestyle. You can choose to be a drunkard, a prominent community member, a vagabond or a God—fearing believer. It's your choice how you live your life.

- It is not what happens to you that matters, but how you choose to respond to what happens to you.

You can have the spirit and the courage of an eagle by being optimistic, making conscious or unconscious choices about your life.

Eagles don't mate before they trust

The eagle is not born married like other birds are. It must look for a partner who cannot be found easily. It must be the only partner as it is a monogamist.

When the male eagle takes interest in the female eagle, a game between a male and a female eagle begins. This game could last for days. The female eagle picks a stick up holding it in its beak, flies up in the air. As soon as it reaches approximately 5km above the surface of the earth, it drops the stick. The male is expected to follow the female in order to keep track of the dropping point of the stick and she requires the male eagle to catch the stick before it touches the ground. The male eagle has to return the stick back to the female.

The female eagle, will fly a little lower and faster with a heavier stick.

Once he has done so successfully after he has been tested again and again with the stick being dropped from different altitudes, the female flies ***less than***

one hundred and fifty metres from the ground and she drops the stick. If the male eagle fails to catch the stick before it reaches the ground the female eagle will chase the male eagle off. If the male eagle succeeds in catching the stick on time the female eagle accepts him and marriage vows are made while both of them being suspended 3000 to 5000 metres in the air. They do this by locking their talons together, both eagles screaming. From that day onwards they will be together for life. Only death will separate them. By catching the stick, the male eagle has satisfied the requirement of a suitable husband who when they have baby eaglets he will be able to catch the eaglets when teaching them to fly.

It has always been my prayer and wish that the human race could be able to stand against the harsh storms of life which makes man fails to stand the vigorous test of time.

How many marriages last for at least ten years? Is it because people choose wrong partners or is it because people settle for marriage before they trust?

Trust is basis of all relationships and it's important to test before we trust a friend or even a prospective partner. The foundation of trust is mutual respect for one another and recognition and acceptance of differences. Trust between partners takes time to develop. Trust and integrity are closely tied. In our daily lives we should not make a mistake of not testing people properly before trusting them.

It is the matter of attitude and choice. The eagle makes the correct choice. One of the most important characteristic of eagles is the possession of an uncommon great attitude. Their attitude determines their altitude. Nothing will distract their focus.

Eagles will always strive to complete what they started. It is not their style to leave an unfinished business.

In this world there are many starters but very few finishers. Because of their attitude and choices they make, they start but don't complete their studies, they start but don't complete their projects, they leave everything hanging. Only a few take a consistent action to achieve their goals. If you combine patience with hard work like eagles do, you will be very happy in the long run. It will be gratifying to see the culmination of all your efforts coming together.

We are living in the world of bleeding and wounded people. People who manifest bitterness in their daily lives as they are driving their cars in the streets. Road rage is the order of our daily lives in my country South Africa. This is caused by people's attitudes. Some of these people choose not to drive before they are drunk.

Some choose to be angry the moment they get behind the steering wheel of their cars. Some choose to disregard every road sign and disrespect other road users.

You have the power right now, to choose what and who you want to be in future. Never ever let hard days derail you and get you off your path to success. Don't blame your past for your present problems, even God cannot change your past. But He can help you in the present to decide how the rest of your life will be. He holds the morrow: **Psalm 31:15 My times are in your hands.** If you trust Him you will never be disappointed. Everything you say, both positive and negative, is an affirmation of your attitude towards the power of God. Whether you say you can or think you can't depends on you.

That is the power of choice.

Chapter 3

Overcoming the storms of life

Many years ago when I was a young boy looking after my father's cattle, I used to enjoy watching at the birds enjoying the comfort of their natural environment.

At times during the early spring the wind would be blowing vigorously, shaking every creature in that area. Trees would be blown, swinging from side to side. But interestingly, in the very tree whose branches are being swayed from side to side, I would see birds sitting peacefully and singing sweetly as if nothing was happening. Why are these birds not affected? What do they have that which makes them enjoy peace at a rowdy environment?

I later realised that this birds were not affected by the storm that was tormenting every creature at that place.

The eagle and the storm

An eagle has an instinctive ability to sense the approaching storm. Unlike other small birds that run for cover when the storm approaches, the eagle gets ready to venture into a storm. It will fly to a high spot and wait for the storm to arrive. It actually sees the storm as an opportunity. By instinct, it knows how to go through storms. When the storm comes, it sets its wings so that the wind will pick it up and lift it above the storm. Birds are scared of storms, but eagles love storms because it lifts them higher and higher through the wind currents. The eagle has the ability to adjust the body in such a way that it has a way to ride the storm. **It rises on the winds that bring the storm**. Eagles rise above storms, taking advantage of the wind currents to soar high above clouds, enemies and torrents. The eagle is soaring above the storm that is raging below it .Eagles soar out of reach, putting themselves between the storm and the sun to keep close to God. They are close to the stars, far above the fray of destruction.

Life is full of storms and when the storms of life come upon us we should not be devastated but should rise above them by setting our minds and our belief toward God. The storms do not have to overcome us.

It should be our aim even here on earth to be eagle-minded by taking the characteristics of eagles and allow God's power to lift us above the challenges of life. God the almighty can enable us to ride the winds that bring the storms of failure, storms of sickness, storms of poverty, marriage storms, spiritual storms and many other storms that bring disappointment and misery in the lives of the human race.

When storms or challenges of this life torment us, we have the power to overcome them with God on our side.

With our minds fixed on the Lord we can put challenges on the wings of prayer, rise above them and be between these challenges and the sun.

In the struggles and tough times of the journey of our lives we still need to be wholeheartedly committed to achieving success without quitting.

In the life of a Christian the wind represents the Holy Spirit as it's often referred to in the Bible. As Christians we need to allow the Holy Spirit to lift us closer to our Lord Jesus. Like eagles we can ride on the current of the Holy Spirit, instead of relying on our own strength and insight. Through the Holy Spirit we can reach greater heights in our flights and do things that seem impossible in the standard of this world.

We have the authority

I am often fascinated by Traffic Officers with their powers relating to the control of traffic on the roads especially in the busy large metro cities. Each of these fellows chooses a spot in a busy place during the rush hour and establish him/ herself for an hour or two to deal with traffic congestion.

The traffic officer uses his or her hand to direct and control traffic.

At a certain stage I stood and watched the situation. I noticed a very tiny officer with his lean hand up. Bringing busses and big trucks to a standstill. Both these vehicles were driven by hefty drivers. They however, obeyed this lean and tiny hand. I then started understanding the authority behind the hand of the traffic officer. Behind the lean and tiny hand of that officer lies the authority of the country. This tiny hand holds the traffic laws of the country. You dare disregard or ignore that hand, you might find yourself in jail or standing in front of the judge of the land. Even the hefty driver respects and obeys the directions given by this tiny officer. ***Wherever these officers are ,the law of the land is with them.***

As children of God we have been given the authority to deal with the storms and challenges facing the human race in the journey of our lives.

When our Lord Jesus Christ gave us a Great Commission, He also gave us this promise: **Matthew (NIV) 28:18 and 20. All authority in heaven and on earth has been given to me. 20 . . . and teaching them to obey everything I commanded you. And surely I am with you always, to the end of the age.**

Many of us are too scared of the heights and strong winds to an extent that we miss the opportunity to see and experience the wonders of the whole new world out there. We are meant to soar up in the sky like the eagle, with our Lord on our side. But unfortunately most of us are unaware of the fact that we are meant for greater things like the eagle are. We are shying away from challenges that are opportunities for us to develop ourselves, our characters and drawing strength from such experiences.

Your thoughts, your dreams and your words have power to create conditions in your life. Your tongue holds the keys of life and death.

You have the authority. As a result , everything you say, positive or negative confirms that.

"Watch your thoughts, for they become words. Choose your words, for they become actions. Understand your actions, for they become habits. Study your habits, for they will become your character. Develop your character, for it becomes your destiny."—Anonymous.

Chapter 4

The eagle and change

Many years ago I read about a man who was driving his beautiful car heading to his destination. He had to arrived on time and therefore his car was to move faster than it did. He tried to drive faster but the lower he pushed the peddle of his car to the floor, the easier the other cars overtook him. Eventually his car was behind all the cars on that road. He then decided to go via the filling station. He enquired from the experienced drivers from the petrol station, what the problem might be with his car.

The answer he got was not difficult. He was informed that there was nothing wrong with his car, but something wrong with his way of driving. He was informed, "at 60 kilometres an hour shift to the second gear."

First gear mentality was no longer relevant to his situation. He had to change. If you do not want to change, change will change you the hard way.

How many people are still dominated by first gear mentality and do not accept that they need to change. Perhaps first gear mentality has served us well in the past but not now. When change comes, we need to take a decision to also change.

I have not stayed long enough in an area where eagles are found. I could therefore not observe the lifespan of eagles. But the researches I have made about the eagle indicate that the eagle has the longest life-span of its' species.

It can live up to 70 years. But to reach that age, the eagle must make a hard choice in its' 40's. At this age the body of the eagle has become overgrown with feathers, its wings can't move as well as before and it's talons and beak are full of calcium deposit and have become useless. This is the wilderness time for the eagle as he has no strength to fly.

The eagle is left with only two options: die or go through a painful process of change lasting for 150 days.

The process requires that the eagle flies to a mountain top in which it was raised on, and sit on its nest. The eagle knocks its beak against a rock until it plucks it out, then it plucks out its talons. Lastly the eagle plucks out its old-aged feathers.

After five months, the eagle takes its majestic flight again and lives for 30 more years. The eagle has undergone the process of renewal as stated in ***"Isaiah 40:31,But they that wait upon the LORD shall renew their strength; they shall mount up with wings as eagles; they shall run, and not be weary; and they shall walk, and not faint."***

At this stage the eagle again relates to the rock by knocking its beak against it. ***"I will love Thee, O Lord my strength.***

The Lord is my Rock, and my fortress, and my deliverer; my God, my strength, in whom I trust; my buckler, and the horn of my salvation, and my high tower." Ps 18:1,2. From the rock it's where the eagle's ultimate hope derives.

There comes a time in our lives when all the life activities become a burden. Obstacles of life make us lose interest, feel hopeless or tired enough to retire from life itself. At this stage we need motivation which will keep the fire inside to force our engine keep functioning and pushing us forward towards achieving our goals. It is in our social, spiritual, emotional and intellectual lives that we need to keep our fire igniting.

God wants us to humble ourselves, acknowledge our weaknesses and confess that we are sinners and that we really have no strength without him and go back to the rock of ages where our salvation comes from. Our Lord Jesus Christ.

In His presence we can then start that renewal process, just as the eagle does when he goes through the renewal process. He is the only one who can renew our strength.

There are some of our past traditions, habits and memories that we need to get rid of. Like eagles, Christians need to go through a renewal period sometime in our lives, and be freed from the past burdens so that we can take advantage of the present and focus to the future with our Lord on our side.

Change is always uncomfortable to accept in our lives but very eminent. Nothing changes like change. For us to survive in our leadership, spiritual lives, social lives and family lives we need to expect and accommodate change.

We live in the world which is different from the world in which we grew. We are parenting children who have never known the world without television, the world without a computer and cell phone.

We therefore need to identify with today's world or else we'll be strangers in our own countries.

First gear mentality should not have a space in our lives. We need to be sober-minded enough so as to be able to shift to the next gear if needs be.

Chapter 5

The road to success is paved with determination

The road to success is **lonely**, the road to success needs a **vision**, the road to success demands **focus and promptness.**

Successful people are doing what everyone else is not.

Successful people care when others don't.

Successful people pay attention to details that others disregard.

Successful people learn from their failure, while others simply learn failure."

The road to success is lonely.

Eagles always fly alone at high altitude. The eagle it's the symbol of power, triumph, royalty and omniscience. It flies alone at high altitude where other small birds cannot. It flies alone unlike other species that flock. Eagles don't fly in V-formation like other birds do. There is no bird that can fly to the height of the eagle. The eagle depends on its own strength and the storm that lifts it up. It takes determination to fly alone at high altitude. This signifies strength and independence. This calls for setting high standards even if there is no one near to those standards.

Instead of turning around when the wind is moving against the eagle, it faces it and draws strength from it. Eagles are made to fly in the high places, out of sight of the naked human eye and out of reach of enemies.

The road to success is lonely. At the top of the mountain you are alone and you have to pay the price with blood and sweat. So you must be ready to make sacrifices to get successful. If you are doing the same thing as everyone else, you're not going to be successful. The ladder of success is not crowded on the upper rung like it is on the lower rung. The road to the achievement of a goal it's lonely with no friends, but you need to keep going when you feel like there is no hope.

The road to success needs a vision

Eagle has a strong vision.

Eagle's eyes can see distances. They can see ahead of them and to the side at the same time.

They can see what other birds do not see. Eagles can see a movement of a rabbit sometimes as far as 5 kilometres away. They can see a tiny lizard on a rock at more than three hundred metres and can see the movement of a fish under water. The Bible confirms this better ***Job39: 27-29—NIV—Does the eagle soar at your command and build his nest on high? He dwells on a cliff and stays there at night; a rocky crack is his stronghold. From there he seeks out his food; his eyes detect it from afar.***

They can also look directly into the sun without being blinded. The Eagle also has a second eyelid that allows them to look directly into the sun! The Eagle is also born with what are called pectin's in their eyes. This unusual gift acts as a homing device for the Eagle. Like a GPS this allows the Eagle to find their way back home even from distances of thousands of kilometres away.

When they are away from their nest there is a certain amount of pain and pressure in their eyes and as they get closer to home it decreases. This gives them an instinct to always want to return to their nest. With its sharp vision, the eagle has the ability to spot a prey and focus on it. The vision of the eagle is highly regarded by the human race.

Many leaders , in their leadership wish to emulate the vision of an eagle. Leadership through the eyes of an eagle is their ultimate target.

Proverbs 29: 18 KJV Where there is no vision, the people perish . . .

Whatever we do in life we need to have a vision or else we'll fail to reach our destination. If you do not have a vision of who you want to be, how you want to succeed or what you want out of life, you are going to lack enthusiasm and your life will lack focus. A vision is a picture or an idea you have in your mind of yourself, your career, or anything relating to your future.

A vision helps you to focus and create a purpose that becomes your measurement for your success. Yes, the vision must be big and focused. Our vision and focus are like a magnet that attracts and connects all the pieces together. Having a vision is the most important thing in the person's path to a successful life. A vision is to inspires you in reaching something that you want. A vision is the most powerful way to keep you focused on your goal of life while keeping you motivated in achieving it. If you don't have a vision you are closing your mind from many possibilities and a brighter and bigger future. Having a vision you will be able to pursue dreams and achieve goals. Hold on to your dreams, for you to achieve the endless possibilities of the future.

The road to success demands focus and promptness.

Eagles see and seize opportunities

The average flight speed of a bald eagle is 56-70 kilometres per hour, it's diving speed is around 120-160km/h. The average speed of the golden eagle is 28-32 kilometres per hour. The Golden eagle is extremely swift when it sees a prey, and can dive at speeds of more than 150 miles (241 kilometres) per hour.

Golden eagles use their speed and talons to snatch up rabbits , marmots and ground squirrels. The eagle is a symbol of strength. It is a fierce fighter. Eagles have even been known to attack an adult deer, bears, foxes and wolves. That is why the eagle is considered the lion of the air. It is the king of the birds just as the lion is the king of beasts.

Eagles are known for the effective manner in which they surprise and overwhelm their target on the ground.

When an eagle spots a prey it narrows its focus on it and set out to get it. No matter the obstacles, the eagle will not move his focus from the prey until it grabs it. Eagles are focused irrespective of whatever thing which might come in the way. Once they set their target, there is very small chance that the prey can escape. Most of the eagles decapitate their prey.

Regardless of what is going on in the world including challenges that present themselves, a vision helps you to focus on what you want to do and why you are doing that which you are doing.

A focus will help you to overcome obstacles in the way and help you hold on when times are tough. Many people lose focus due to the fact that they lack vision. The eagle is very prompt at seizing an opportunity when a prey is sited.

Procrastination is a thief of time. Many people are not prompt at grabbing an opportunity when it presents itself. There are many chronic procrastinators who are ever late in doing what they are set to do. Very few people are leading the life they wish to live and doing what they want to do at the time they wish to.

But the motivated mind will teach a person how to wipe out procrastination for the rest of his life. They want much more but don’t know how to get it or make it happen.

Successful people, are different from unsuccessful and unhappy people. They think differently, act differently, and play by entirely different set of rules from the rest. They get what they want because they know how to get what they want due to their motivated focus.

Are you where you want to be in your professional career and personal life? Are you the person you always hoped you would become? If not ,do you know the reason why? When you know the secret of success you can have everything you want in life.

Chapter 6

Eagles are very patient

I studied about eagles and their personality traits and realised that there are personality traits that were inherent in the eagle that God wants us to have in our lives.

The eagle is known for its patience, especially when it has spotted a prey that disappeared from the scene. At times a rabbit which has been targeted as a prey would go hiding in a hole for more than an hour before he comes out of his hiding place. Once he does, the eagle will at a lightning speed seize the opportunity, and swoop down to catch him within a moment. The eagle is then rewarded with a good meal.

When the male eagle was proposing a marriage relationship to the female eagle, a lot of patience was exercised during the twig game. The male eagle was finally rewarded with a life partner.

During the renewal period of an eagle a lot of patience needs to be exercised for at least hundred and fifty days before the eagle can regain its strength. The eagle is then rewarded with an extra thirty years of lifespan. The eagle does not just fly, it does some calculations.

He has to learn to be able to soar without flapping his wings, and this needs patience. He needs patience to wait for wind thermals to come up on him. A wind thermal is a big gust of wind that will rise up from the atmosphere.

During these days of speed, we also need the patience of an eagle. Patience will lead us to self-discipline which will in turn help prevent mistakes that might bring disappointments in our lives. Patience inculcates discipline.

Perhaps it will be imperative to give a short definition of patient.

Noah Webster defines patient as persevering or waiting with calmness. If you wait with calmness you will not act until you are sure that you have calculated your intended action correctly.

With patience you will be able to discover what's important in life. When people mature, their values change. The willingness to wait, teaches people what truly matters to them. Patience helps you practice caution in everything you do.

The world we now live in, with everything done at breakneck speed which causes a lot of stress, requires patience.

Patience is more than a virtue, it is a powerful weapon. A virtue is the quality of moral excellence, righteousness, and responsibility. You don't need to go to school and pass an examination on virtues. But for you to be successful, you need virtues.

For us to be patient we need divine intervention. Because one of the nine fruits of the Holy Spirit is the fruit of patience. For the human race to be able to live with one another in the workplace, community, church as well as our own families we need patience more than anything else.

This is one of the main qualities and traits of the eagle, and this quality must perfectly line up with what God would like to have inculcated into our personality traits so that we can become good and mighty soldiers of our Lord Jesus Christ.

The patience of an eagle will bring sober-mindedness in the lives of many. To at least watch the culture of now, which cause many people to lose their future .We need it NOW.

We need to be skinnier NOW, healthier NOW, richer NOW, happier NOW. Living in the culture of now causes people to eat now, spend now and get what you want now and never cast your eyes to the future. Yes many people emphasise perseverance and hard work but overlook patience. More than just an attribute to be cultivated, patience is an energetic experience.

Lack of patience contributes to accidents that occur in our roads, students who fail to complete their studies at different institutions, the broken families which were caused by failed marriages, political parties that are mushrooming every year, division of churches that is happening on daily basis and the cold war that is taking place in the churches. This cold war causes our churches to be cold and lack the Holy Spirit.

Young adults in my country lack patience. They want everything, and they want it now. Impatience is very costly and leads to lifestyle inflation. The youngsters are used to the standard of living created by their parents for many years.

They can't wait until they can afford similar luxuries. They want to enrich themselves the wrong way.

Patience is very powerful. We practice patience when we are in a convoy during the rush hour, and are in a hurry to reach our destinations. With patience we are able to see when to be still and when to move. All good things come to those who wait. If we are facing in the right direction, all we have to do is keep on walking. We know these things to be true, and practical and there's a part of us that understands it, believes it, feels the wisdom behind it yet another part denies it. But what do we do to get out of this trap? How do we practice patience? How do we make it a reality of our daily lives? What do we do about the part of us that is screaming like a toddler . the part of us which doesn't want to be patient? The part of us that says, "I want it now !"

It pays to be patient but a patient person must realize the value of time.

To realize the value of ONE YEAR , ask a student who failed a grade and has to repeat it. To realize the value of ONE MONTH ask a mother who gave a birth to a premature baby and has to wait to see him grow. To realize the value of ONE WEEK ask the editor of a weekly newspaper who needs to be patient enough to get articles to be published on a specific day. To realize the value of ONE HOUR ask the lovers who are waiting to meet at a stipulated time.

Be patient and discover the deep, calm and quiet power of the experience of patience. That is the POWER of patience.

Teach us, O Lord, the disciplines of patience, for to wait is often harder than to work. Peter Marshall

CHAPTER 7

Eagles only eat live prey

Eagles are very choosy in their eating. They are not like other birds who may go feeding on worms or like the vultures who feed off dirt , mostly dead carcasses. The eagle chooses it's food each day. That is why they are more beautiful than vultures who feed on carcasses. If it wants fish then it goes and finds fish, if it wants squirrel or rabbit then it goes and finds one. An eagle often does not eat what it finds, it finds what it wants to eats. If it wants rabbits or wolves it goes and finds one, if it wants fish it goes for fish.

When an eagle sees it's prey, it swoops down on it, kills it and carries it to it's nest high in the rocks and eat it while it is still warm. They hunt for and kill their own food. An eagles is not a scavenger. He doesn't eat dead food even if he is not sure if its hunting expedition will be a success. This is the Eagle's source of strength. Fresh meat.

It is common knowledge that one's lifespan is partly determined by one's diet. Eagles have the longest lifespan of almost all the creatures of the wild due to the **fresh food it eats**, **excellent relationship skills**, its uncommon **great attitude** and its influential **successful lifestyle.**

The human race needs to be eagle-minded by picking and choosing the best diet for his physical, social, intellectual and spiritual growth and development. He needs to improve his attitude and lifestyle for his lifespan to excel that of an eagle. A tiny country Monaco's life expectancy is almost 90 years for all people. But women live almost 95 years old. Their diet is very healthy.

Researchers have identified five regions in the world where health and longevity go hand in hand. The people who live in these regions do not have special genes that influence their longevity. Though their cultures are not the same, yet all of them share one thing in common that explains the secret of their longevity. These regions are commonly known as Blue zone regions.

Fresh food: There **is** variety of differences in the foods native to each of this regions, but traditional diet in each area is primarily plant-based, with an abundance of fresh fruits and vegetables being eaten daily. Fresh fish is also their common meal. Their diet is very healthy, but also inexpensive. Their eagle-mindedness of keeping to fresh food strengthen their health.

Daily Physical Activity: The eagle is mostly in the air interacting with the storm and hunting in the wild. It has an active lifestyle. People in the regions mentioned above don't have to plan to do constructive exercises, because regular moderate physical activity is a built-in part of their cultures. Their most common form of exercise is walking, even people in their 80s and 90s and older walk kilometres each day as they go about their daily routines. People in these regions work the land or garden on a daily basis. As a result of their daily activities, along with their healthy diets, they are free from chronic illnesses like diabetes and heart disease raging across much of the rest of the world.

Strong Family Bonds**:** In the blue zone regions a family always comes first. Family relationships are loving and caring. Marriages are faithful, and family members tend to live close by each other, creating a nurturing extended family dynamic. Researchers believe that having strong family bonds can add as much as six extra years to a person's life because of the physical and emotional benefits such bonds provide. An eagle is family bound, very close to the spouse and its baby eaglets. It doesn't have the word divorce or post—divorce trauma in its family vocabulary. Eagles can only be separated by death. Praise God!

Participation in Faith-Based Activities: Blue zone people are spiritual and religious, and have a strong connection to respective faiths. Participating in faith-based worship services and other activities is very important to them and is something they do at least once a week. One of the reasons why women live longer than men is the fact that women go to church more than man do.

Participating in faith-based activities with others can increase your lifespan by as much as a decade or more. In South Africa, heart attack is becoming common to men due to the fact that they prefer taverns than churches. Some physical ailments need spiritual healing. The more you fellowship with others, the healthier you will become, and you'll likely discover that you are becoming happier too.

Chapter 8

Life outside the comfort zone

Leaving your comfort zone means pushing your boundaries and trying something new. Your intention is to beat the status quo and conquer your fears. To move into that uncomfortable and foreign environment with an open mind and courage. This means to start living. You cannot start living until you are able to live outside of yourself

When the baby eagles are born high on the mountain , both parents assume responsibility for their care. Like all other babies, eaglets, love to eat and sleep and spend their initial life in the comfort of the nest. They are not in a hurry at all to get out of the nest. Everyday, the mother eagle finds food and drop it directly into the open mouths of the hungry eaglets. But when the time arrives for the baby eaglets to start flying, the mother eagle pulls out all of that fur and those animal skins, as a result those little baby eagles are sitting on thorns.

The mother eagle hovers over the nest and starts fluttering and flapping those powerful wings and that blows all of the loose feathers and fur away from those baby eagles and causing a great commotion. This time, there is no food. After hovering a few rounds, the mother eagle would make a dive into the nest and begin to shake it violently. She then takes one of her babies on her wings and starts soaring into the skies and go up to between 1500 and 2500 metres. By the time the baby eaglet begins to tremble the mother eagle starts swooping and soaring around through the sky and suddenly tips her wings and the little baby eagle falls off and starts to struggle. The baby eaglet starts to do somersaults and flaps his wings as he is heading down to the ground but just before he hits the ground, the mother eagle flies underneath in order to catch the baby and picks him up on her powerful wings and takes him up again to the sky.

This process is repeated over and over again until all the babies learn how to fly. At about the fourteenth to fifteenth try, the eaglet begins to fly.

That is an indirect way the mother eagle teaches the baby eaglets to leave the nest. If the mother eagle would not stir the nest, the eaglets would remain in the nest the rest of their lives. The fear of the unknown would also stop them from learning how to fly. It is no point being an eagle that cannot fly.

We are living in the world in which many people are full of fear. Fear is an emotion caused by anticipated danger, it is caused by the unknown. When we have fear, we will do or avoid doing anything to feel safer. *Some people fear death, some fear failure, some fear being alone, some fear success, some fear going to hell, and some fear, fear itself.* Fear limits our freedom of facing challenges, keeps us from pursuing our dreams and prevents us from reaching our true potential.

Fear limits our ability to fly to the level God wants us to fly. God wants us to become all that he intends for us to become.

We can get very comfortable in our respective nests where we find ourselves. And get very complacent and satisfied with where we are and what we are. And fear may cause us to regard challenges as the plan of the devil . Challenges are not caused by the devil but our Lord who allows our nest to be shaken because He wants us to grow into maturity, as we are made to fly. The Bible says **in Exodus 19:4 NIV84** that God carried the children of Israel on eagles' wings and brought them to Himself. In this verse the eagle symbolizes God. God treats His children the way mother eagle treats her young babies. God is always close to His children. In the same way the mother eagle teaches her babies to fly on their own , God teaches us to use faith by believing in His word.

In the book of ***Deuteronomy 32 :11 HIV 84*** God says to the Israelites: ***Like an eagle that stirs up its nest and hovers over its young, that spreads its wings to catch them and carries them on its pinions.***

"He will carry the children of Israel on eagle's wings." But we need to be prepared to move out of our comfort zones. Our comfort zones define the way we do things, our old way of thinking, our values and our way of living.

When God comes and stirs up our nest, we are overwhelmed by fear.

He always stirs up our nest with a purpose and a good reason. We need to move beyond our comfort zone.

Beyond the comfort zone there is growth. Beyond the comfort zone we can stand on God's word. Beyond the comfort zone I can learn to spread my wings. I can learn to fly. When hard times come, God will carry me through all my challenges. But if we don't leave our comfort zones we will fail as there is no survival in the comfort zone.

Chapter 9

Eagles don't take their mates for granted

The eagle is known to be having a very good relationship skills due to their great attitude. After their twig game, eagles make their marriage vows. The marriage vows of the eagles are made three to five thousand metres in the air. This ceremony is done by locking talons together and turning head over heels with both eagles screaming with joy. Eagles are totally committed to their mates. ***They will remain together for life, In good times or bad, in sickness and in health, till death does them part.*** Eagles remain together until one of them dies, then the survivor can only be in a position to accept a new mate who is not attached to any other eagle.

After marriage the eagles seek for an appropriate location to begin to build their home. They look for a high inaccessible location with their backs turned to a rock wall which cannot be reached by the predators. There is no divorce in the vocabulary of the family of eagles. The human race? How is our relationship?

The divorce rate for all the marriages in the world now stands at about 50% while second and third marriage face a divorce rate of 60%. Statistics now show that 67% of recent marriages now end in divorce. In South Africa only, in 2008 the divorce rate for various racial groups stood as follows: Africans 35%, Indians/Asians 6.2%, mixed groups 3,1% whilst that of White groups is 32,8%.

This is an indication that as long as we still have so many people globally, whose marriages cannot last for as long as they live, then an eagle is still our role model.

Unlike human beings, eagles can adjust quickly and with great accuracy to any situation. What a difference to the world this would make if human beings, could make such a commitment to their families! Couples should consider making marital adjustments immediately after their wedding day. This could improve their commitment to each other. In my experience I have realized that the marital adjustments mentioned in the next paragraph can strengthen our families.

They are not once-off but life time adjustments.

Social adjustments: Man is a gregarious animal created by God for fellowship with himself and with one another. Couples discover that differences in social likes and dislikes that they never dreamed existed, will emerge after marriage. During their courtship days their love for each other overshadow their awareness to their social differences. Interpersonal relationship play a major role in a marriage relationship. The experience they have had in their social relationships in the past, can develop willingness to co-operate with each other , and be able to easily adjust to their marriage. Being rational creatures we can cultivate new likes and dislikes by enthusiastically getting ourselves into something for peace love's sake.

Financial adjustments: This adjustment is perhaps the most important, because most couples have been financially independent or dependent upon their parents. If the wife has been working prior to marriage and kept her own account, she may wish to do the same after marriage. Many people find financial adjustments very difficult. Who should handle the money?

Friction may develop if the non-working wife expects her husband to share the financial work load. The young couple's patience and joyous acceptance of their financial capabilities can lead to a long-lasting and happy marriage.

Sexual adjustments: This is one of the unspeakable major marriage adjustment problems. Sexual adjustment determine the intimacy and the happiness of a couple. It is the one most likely to lead to a marital discord and unhappiness if it is not satisfactorily achieved. A high percentage of divorces are caused by sexual adjustments.

In-law Adjustments: Your relationship with your partner's family is important. Young couples must learn to adjust to their in-laws if they are to avoid frictional relationship with their spouses. Most parents find it difficult to adjust after the marriage of their children, even though they know they should. Mothers often have greater difficulty parting with their sons than fathers do to their daughters. In-law problems are eased if the marriage is between persons of the same religions or culture. Eagles let go of their eaglets, they allow them their independence.

Above anything else , as a couple, ask God for wisdom on how to live with the person who is different from you. Like an eagle, married couples should possess singleness of mind and a great sense of purpose for their families. Once eagles get their partners, they will stay true and loyal to each other for life.

In this day and age, where 50% of all marriages are ending up in a divorce court , once God leads us to the person we should marry He will expect us to stay true, loyal and faithful to each other to the day we die.

If the church, the Bride of Christ, could make such a commitment to God and their spouses as eagles do to their mates, this would be a very good world to live in and this would really please God! As eagle-minded Christians, we should do the same, with God on our side.

More than anything else ***a man shall leave his father and mother and be joined to his wife and they shall be one flesh Gen 2:24.*** The foundation is ***Leave, Cleave*** and ***be one flesh***.

Chapter 10

Moral degeneration

Moral degeneration is the deterioration or decline of the standard of behaviour, or the decline of the principles of right and wrong. There are a lot of social evils caused by the fall of man. There is a warfare declared by some religious leaders, some politicians, community leaders and other morally sensitive people against these evils but we don't seem to be winning. Some minor battles seem to be won but it looks like we are losing the warfare. This is a spiritual warfare that is happening behind the scenes of everyday life and needs divine intervention.

Our newspapers and electronic media reports distress both the readers and the listeners. Bad news are actually good news. News without bad news it's no news at all.

Adults are meant to be the role models of the youth, but how many are still leading an exemplary life. Very few indeed and they seem to be a square pack in a round hole. It has become normal for a teacher to have sexual relationships with innocent underage learners and get away with it.

It is no longer surprising to find a sixty year old in bed with a seventeen year old. Both men and women are involved in molesting the young ones. A punishment for those who rape little children is far from befitting the crime they committed.

Members of public expect a high standard of integrity among the police officers. When we are in trouble we run to them for help. They are supposed to be our ultimate hope when things are bad. But newspaper headlines go on and on about police officers committing crimes and becoming part of criminal elements. Cops commit crimes from dealing with drugs to committing burglaries and armed robberies, kerb crawling and perverting the course of justice.

Where are these officers? Hundreds of them are still serving despite their criminal convictions. Some victims run away from criminals, to seek protection from the cops only to discover that they are running from one criminal to the another. There are some dangerous criminals out there than some of those who are in jail.

They are white collar criminals. They are running with the hare and hunting with the hounds.

South Africa is one of the countries with very high HIV/Aids prevalence. In the last six to seven years I have seen both public and private sectors running HIV/Aids awareness programmes. Many teachers registered with Universities to acquire qualifications related to this scourge. Many precautions to avoid HIV/Aids are taken. One of these precautions is good morals, being honest to one's partner. The horrors of this disease is laid bare in pamphlets and lectures, nothing is hid. But a marked improvement in morals has not been noted. The standard of our morals leaves much to be desired.

Politicians give policy statements regarding good principles of behaviour but some of them have been seen interacting with prostitutes, enriching themselves the wrong way while the poorest of the poor are starving.

Our standard of education seem to be lowering year after year. But politicians deny that. There are laws preventing the sale of alcohol to the under age children.

But these laws are not being enforced in the townships and rural areas.

Drug abuse has grown to near epidemic proportions. Drug abuse in South Africa grows to unimagined levels. Drug related crimes dominate the agenda of many meetings. The very young are the victims of drug abuse and statistics show that the incidence of pre-teenage addiction in some areas is becoming a significant problem. Teenage pregnancy is in most cases related to drug abuse.

Marriage is no longer guided by love, but by fame and riches. Some youngsters are looking for rich and celebrated partners. Even if they can be married for only one month it's fine. Nobody can tell them that getting in such a relationship you are turning yourself into a commodity. Nobody can tell them that life is not only about money and riches but also about integrity, respect and dignity. Yes that is moral degeneration, marked by crime without punishment, schools without discipline, children without fathers, reward without effort, rights without responsibilities, behaving as if life ends up at the grave yard, people with twisted morals and indifference to right and wrong.

Our country and the world at large needs moral regeneration.

Christ, not politics, is capable of saving the world. Christ, not actions that symbolize life and health, will heal the world and keep it clean.

One of the very powerful traits of the eagle is that they are very bold, courageous, and powerful and the eagle's deadly enemy is the serpent. Eagles are able to engage with poisonous snakes and tearing their heads off with their beak or an eagle will carry the serpent high up and drop him on a rock a couple of times until he dies. God wants us to take an example from the eagle. As the eagle is the most powerful and feared bird in the sky, God wants us to be fearless, trust in Him and engage with the spiritual warfare that is causing moral degeneration in South Africa and the world at large. We should not fear any demonic or any evil people as God will always protect us. As eagle—minded Christians we will always have to deal with our main enemy , the devil. God has given Christians spiritual gifts to defeat the enemy and use the word of God as a rock to destroy, crush and defeat the devil.

Chapter 11

The power of example

The example through the eyes of a child

Raising children is a very challenging, responsible and gratifying task parents can face. There is no manual or formal training that can help parents to bring up their children. Our way of bring up children is influenced by who we are, our values and views, our surroundings and our own upbringing. In most cases patterns from the parent's own social experiences are repeated and passed on to their children.

I wish to tell the story of a certain sociable man who loved visiting a tavern two kilometres away from his home. He walked to this tavern every Saturday evening. He would spend half a night with his friends, socializing and having some drinks. At midnight he would return home, make a lot of noise, sing, dance and play with his two year old boy. This little boy enjoyed his dad's friendliness which seemed obvious every Saturday evening.

One Saturday night while this man was still enjoying his drinks with his mates his little boy got in and went straight to him. There were no children at that spot.

Dad got frightened on seeing this young fellow because the way to the tavern was complicated and a bit distant for the two year old unaccompanied child.

"Boy, how did you come here, who showed you the way?" asked the man.

"I carefully followed your footprints from home to this place" answered the boy. Children can learn from us just by watching. Our children are watching us, doing as we do more than as we say. Parents are the most influential role models children have. When parents show kindness, respect, friendliness, hospitality, humbleness, and generosity to people, their children will behave in the same way. When parents are proud and pompous, their children are likely to be the same. Bringing up children four aspects need to be balanced—***love, discipline, teaching and example.***

Discipline without love degenerates into an abuse, love without

discipline leads to a warped personality. Teaching without an example

leads to a shallow understanding and an example without teaching

leads to a partial understanding.

Above all the power of an example cannot be underestimated. It is the best way to teach, because it is through seeing you live your testimony that others can gain their own testimony. The eagle does not tell the eaglets what to do when it wants to teach it how to fly, it only removes it from its comfort zone and pushes the eaglet out of the nest. After rescuing the eaglet several times from falling to the ground the eaglet has already learnt what is expected of him. The eagle expects results from the baby eaglet after setting a clear example to it. The eagle is a good teacher who teaches by setting an example.

The example of a teacher is the easiest book which can even be read by the laziest child.

Parents should be very careful about the example they are setting to their children. Both fathers and mothers need to read this message:

Walk A Little Plainer, Daddy

Walk a little plainer, Daddy,
Said a little boy so frail.
I'm following in your footsteps,
And I don't want to fail.
Sometimes your steps are very plain,
Sometimes they are hard to see,
So walk a little plainer, Daddy,
For you are leading me.

I know that once you walked this way
Many years ago,
And what you did along the way,
I'd really like to know.
For sometimes when I am tempted,
I don't know what to do.
So walk a little plainer, Daddy,
For I must follow you.

Someday when I'm grown up,
You are like I want to be.
Then I will have a little boy,
Who will want to follow me.
And I would want to lead him right,
And help him to be true.
So walk a little plainer, Daddy.
For we must follow you.

Author Unknown

Not only children want to see an example from their parents and other adults, some adults too want to see an example from political leaders, community leaders, teachers and spiritual leaders. If you do not set a good example for your children they will get role models from the streets. Christians should be very careful in walking their talk and talking their walk.

Here is the story of a very committed young Christian in my area. He was very active in his church and did not want to do anything that was against his Christian principles.

When he got married, his wedding was one of the most blessed and exemplary weddings in his church. There were a number of things he was taught not to do as a Christian because doing them was a sin. One of the things he was told not to do was drinking liquor. For him a mere touching of a glass of wine was a sin.

In his wedding, a highly regarded bishop of his church was called to come and grace the occasion and propose a toast.

His bishop was not living in the same area with him. The good bishop instructed everybody at the tables to pour wine in their classes and a toast was proposed to the success of their marriage. The bishop made them drink a little wine in their glasses. Everyone was happy and the wedding continued to the end and the young man took his wife and continued with life.

Five years later the bishop organized a revival at the area, during the day he did open—air preaching on the streets. He met someone at the shopping complex who was very drunk. This drunkard knew him because he addressed him as bishop. The preacher took pains in trying to convince this man how biblically wrong was it to be a drunkard. But the man reminded the bishop that, he hated drinking as a Christian but on his wedding day, the bishop showed him how correct was it to drink. Since that day the man drank until he graduated into a heavy drunkard who eventually could not control his drinking habits.

That is the power of example. On this man's wedding day, the bishop did not explain why was wine used for toasting and how and when is it biblically wrong to engage in drinking. This caused the young Christian to backslide.

Christ has set us an example to follow as his children.***1Peter 2:21 For even hereunto were ye called: because Christ also suffered for us, leaving us an example, that ye should follow his steps.***

Chapter 12

If you want to know my Glory, know my story.

I was born and bred in a farm where education was foreign to the people who lived in it. I am from the family of ten.

I was brought up in a cultural environment with very strong family values. My grandfather was a clan leader, a traditional healer and a law-giver in our clan. My youngest uncle died in an accident that occurred in his place of employment a few months after he got married. I was still four years old. Ancestral worship and traditional healers were at the centre of our faith and belief system.

My duties as a young boy.

I grew up a very sickly boy from the age of five. I developed a chest disease, daily headache, knee dislocation, and a nose bleeding which could not be cured. Despite these infirmities I was given the responsibility of looking after my father's sheep, goats and cattle from the age of five. A boy of that age was not expected to stay at home irrespective of his health.

The word school, did not exist in the vocabulary of the residence of our farm. The farm in which we lived belonged to a white farmer. Once a year each household had to get one representative to go and work at the farm without any remuneration. It was an indirect slavery practiced during the apartheid years.

As a young herdsboy I was consistently exposed to dangerous situations in our grazing fields. It was my duty together with the other boys in that farm to take our herds to the graze fields, about five kilometres away from home. We would leave at seven in the morning and return around two or three in the afternoon. As young boys we consistently ducked and dived to avoid various dangerous snakes. As we were walking barefooted, one day I stepped over dry bones of a snake. Pierced by the bones of a snake was the most painful feeling I've ever experienced in my life. They are not only poisonous but more painful than a thorn.

My elder brother came to fetch me and gave me a ride on his bicycle as I could not walk. I was not even taken to the hospital. My grandfather used his sharp knife to cut my swollen foot open, removed pieces of broken bones and gave me an anti-poison portion as he was a traditional healer.

Gang fighting was very rife among herdsboys as it proved strength and bravery. I did not easily retreat even when my rivals were stronger than us. As a result one day my rival group set a dog on me. I was terribly attacked by their dog. Actually one side of my bum was almost bitten off by the dog. It was very easy to be bitten by a dog at that part of the body as we did not wear trousers but skins.

My father had to arrange with the owner of the dog to get its fur. The fur was burned, and my wound was exposed to the smoke produced by the burning fur.

This was done in order to weaken the poison or the infection which might be caused by the dog's bite. I stayed at home until I was partly healed. There was no treatment from the hospital, only natural herbs were used to clean my wound. Thanks God, from that day onwards I was allowed to graduate from skins to wear a trouser.

When I was ten years of age, a school was established in our farm. The school was housed in our family thatched roofed wagon shelter. It was a blessing for me and my siblings to start schooling in this Missionary school without buildings. The school was controlled by the apartheid Dutch Reformed church ministers of religion who hired and fired teachers as they wished. When a learner was absent for three weeks from the Sunday school class he or she was dismissed from school. I was at this school up to Grade four and had to look for another school to further my studies.

After completing my Grade four ,sickly as I was my father bought me a bicycle and sent me to the Lutheran church missionary school forty kilometers away from home. Thanks God I am still alive. That was a very strenuous ride. I was frequently exposed to thunder and lightning because of the distance. The following year my younger brother joined me. We were exposed to severe winter cold conditions, as we were riding our bicycles barefooted and without hand-gloves. It is not easy to leave home at six in the morning and return at five in the evening without a lunch box.

I always felt pity for my younger brother who used to daydream about the possibility of getting a lot of money to buy a car and drive to school.

Drinking tea was a luxury we could only afford ones a month. Bread could only be eaten twice or thrice a year due to poverty and distances from shops. It would take one the whole day to go to the nearest shop.

I did my junior secondary school education 80 kilometres away from home as secondary schools were very few those days. When I was in Grade 9 my father died. He was poisoned while he paid relatives a condolence visit. I then remained with no one to help me further my education. I was exposed to relatives who had no interest in education. I was instead forced to go to the initiation school to obtain my manhood. When I graduated from the initiation school I still felt thirsty for education. I went back to school. I became a laughing stock because during those days men did not go to school, only boys did.

At the age of nineteen, I accepted Christ as my Lord and Saviour. Glory to God, all the sicknesses which tormented me for more than fourteen years disappeared. The bleeding problem which lasted for hours, a headache which would torment me every afternoon, the chest disease which would come every two weeks and knees that would dislocate anytime became a thing of the past through prayer and faith.

I went to the boarding school to do Matriculation. And I joined a very powerful prayer group which helped me to grow spiritually and experienced the power of God in all my daily activities.

The challenge I had is when during the school holidays I found the traditional healer at home. She demanded white chicken about five or six of them, she cut their heads off and when this headless chickens jumped about before they died she was ullulating. This woman would take the blood, mix it with her herbs but take all the chicken to her home 300 kilometres away. I refused to use her herbs and to be cut by her as a sign of protection and refused to be taken to the grave yard for ancestral worship. I was a prayerful boy. Thanks God that my rebellion paid dividend to the whole family, though it took a number of years.

During the school holidays I used to work to get money for my school fees.

At times I would move from village to village selling oranges to get money. As God was on my side I completed both my Matriculation and my teaching diploma.

Perhaps I need to shorten the details of my story. But I need to mention that the qualifications I acquired, that is the two diplomas, four degrees including my PhD were obtained on part time basis. I must attribute my success to my family values and Christian principles.

This world is a jungle in which one can easily get lost. Those who survive are those who do not try to find themselves but create themselves. I did not want to find myself among the pleasure centred people, I did not want to find myself among the drunkards, I did not want to find myself amongst the people who will try to define me who I am, I did not want to find out from other people who, how and what I am and what I can be. I instead decided to create myself.

A day has 24 hour divided into three shifts. The first 8 hours is for us to work as God commanded us, the second 8 hours is for sleeping, to have rest for the next day. The last 8hours is for practicing our power of choice. It is this last 8 hours that one can use to either destroy himself, improve his life, do a lot of lazing or create yourself. I prefer to be a self-made man, a self-created man because God created me for a purpose in this world.

An eagle has a great sense of purpose. It perseveres through difficulties. Before the eagle could go to the rock for renewal, he sits helplessly in the valley. Other merciful eagles drop him some food until he gains strength to get to the top of the rock for renewal. If he fails to get food from the merciful ones who have gone through the same process he will surely die.

Chapter 13

Finish what you started

Starting something is often easy, but finishing is usually much harder. Do you finish what you start? Do you have inner strength to go through with the projects you have started? Do you think before you start doing something?

It has always been my concern that many people start doing things with courage and enthusiasm, then after a while they lose enthusiasm and energy to continue. The excuses they give would be lack of time or too much work to do. At times we do things in response to something we saw someone doing, so when enthusiasm wanes we quit. It is important to develop self-discipline and perseverance which will in turn build self—confidence and faith in us. This will enable us to start and finish things that require more effort.

Dreams are often very difficult to finish because they involve longer timeframes and unless you have self—discipline and perseverance, you often do not have a finish line.

It is interesting that eagles build until they finish their nest. They are not overwhelmed by the intensity of the task, because they have a great sense of purpose, they follow their dream.

Failure to finish what we start makes many people fail to achieve success in life. Perhaps many people ignore their ***dreams***, they don't have **perseverance** and they can' t ***manage their failures***.

Know and achieve your dream

Each of us has a dream placed in the heart. This is a vision deep inside that speaks to our soul. It's the thing we were born to do. It draws on our potential and gifts. It appeals to our highest ideas. It sparks our feelings of destiny. It is in line with our purpose of life. Our dream starts us on our journey of success. A dream gives us direction and focus. Without a dream we may not easily see the potential in ourselves because we don't look beyond our current circumstances.

A dream helps us prioritise, give us hope for the future, and it also brings us power in the present. Make your dream a priority and achieve it despite of the pressures of this life and other daily activities. A dream predicts our future. With a brilliant mental picture we can go from one accomplishment to another with our mind focused into the future. Perhaps some creatures can be a role model to us in pursuing a dream and finishing the work: ***Proverb 30: 25-27(NIV 84) Ants are creatures of little strength, yet they store up their food in summer ; coneys are creatures of little power, yet they make their home in the crags. Locusts have no king, yet they advance together in ranks.*** Yes, something can be learnt from the above little creatures. They have a vision, they are future focused and are organized.

The value of perseverance

According to the Merriam Webster dictionary, Perseverance is a continued effort to do or achieve something despite difficulties, failure or opposition.

Perseverance is an action that we must take and remain steadfast in that action until we achieve the results. For us to finish what we start we need to have perseverance. Perseverance is a very powerful virtue. The power of perseverance is necessary because it is a force that will allow you to push until something happens and be able to fulfill things that you desire, whatever they might be. It is the virtue that allows you to hold on to your dream or desire long enough to establish health habits that enable you achieve success. Keep on keeping on utilising the life changing power of perseverance then things will happen.

Failing successfully

Most of us were taught from an early age that success is good and failure is bad. Consequently, those who give correct answers are rewarded, while disparagement and punishment go to those who give wrong answers.

Two of the deepest entrenched fears of most people, is the fear of man (what other people think) and fear of failure. People are success oriented with deep fear of failure.

People are scared of starting projects because they fear failure. Your mature attitude towards failure is very crucial. The two types of failures is a noble failure and a stupid failure.

To make a mistake once is a pity, but to repeat the same mistake is stupidity. It is necessary to change your attitude towards failure and change your response to failure by accepting responsibility. The most important key to failing successfully is to be on watch and learn why you failed. At times failure is necessary as it leads to success. Failure can teach you about yourself , your strengths and weaknesses. Lessons that can't be taught in any school can be learnt from failure. Henry Ford states that, "Failure is the opportunity to begin again more intelligently , "While Thomas Edison believes that if you fail you've just found 10 000 ways that won't work. We must not fear failure because to the wise, recovering from failure can drastically increase our creativity and ability to do things.

The eagle never looks to the past failures, they always look forward to the future. Eagles will struggle and persevere against all odds. For eagle-minded believers to achieve success they need not live under fear. Success can only be achieved through perseverance and failing successfully.

Success is knowing your purpose in life and growing to reach your potential. Commitment to continual improvement is the key to reaching your potential and to being successful. When God is on our side, our true success is not defined by our achievement, but by our reliance on him. Even in our failures, when we still rely on Him at the time when we are at the bottom of our social ladder , He can surprise us with success.

Chapter 14

The Majesty of the Eagle

I believe that through the eagle God was trying to convey some extra knowledge to us, so that we have an understanding as to what additional qualities He would like us to have worked into our personalities as a human race.

An eagle has a look of royalty and therefore considered Majestic. Christians have the same royalty and are considered Kings and Priests of the Lord because of the death of Christ on the cross. Jesus has given us the Majestic royalty by sacrificing His death on the cross.

I adore the Almighty for the manner in which He created the eagle. I believe behind the name **Eagle** stands the spirit that created it. When the spirit is powerful the word is clothed in that power. Yes the eagle is mentioned so many times in the Bible because of it's importance and influence to the human race.

A number of times an eagle is mentioned in the Bible

In the sections I have read in the Bible, the eagle is mentioned 26 times. It is possible that there might be some verses I have not come across where the eagle is mentioned in the Bible.

1. **Isaiah 40:31** But they that wait upon the LORD shall renew their strength; they shall mount up with wings as **eagles**; they shall run, and not be weary, and they shall walk , and not faint.

2. **Leviticus 11:13** These are the birds you are to detest and not eat because they are detestable: the **eagle**, the vulture and the black vulture,

3. **Leviticus 11:18** And the swan, and the pelican, and the gier **eagle,**

4. **Deuteronomy 14:12** But these you may not eat: the **eagle**, the vulture, the black vulture.

5. **Deuteronomy 14:17** And the pelican, and the gier **eagle**, and the cormorant,

6. **Deuteronomy 28:49** The Lord will bring a nation against you from far away , from the ends of the earth, like an **eagle** swooping down, a nation whose language you will not understand,

7. **Deuteronomy 32:11** As an **eagle** stirreth up her nest, fluttereth over her young, spreadeth abroad her wings, taketh them, beareth them on her wings:

8. **Job 9:26** They are passed away as the swift ships: as the **eagle** that hasteth to the prey.

9. **Job 39:27** Doth the **eagle** mount up at thy command, and make her nest on high?

10. **Psalms 103:5** Who satisfieth thy mouth with good things; so that thy youth is renewed like the **eagle's**.

11. **Proverbs 23:5** Wilt thou set thine eyes upon that which is not? for riches certainly make themselves wings; they fly away as an **eagle** toward heaven.

12. **Proverbs 30:19** The way of an **eagle** in the air; the way of a serpent upon a rock; the way of a ship in the midst of the sea; and the way of a man with a maid.

13. **Jeremiah 48:40** For thus saith the LORD; Behold, he shall fly as an **eagle**, and shall spread his wings over Moab.

14. **Jeremiah 49:16** Thy terribleness hath deceived thee, and the pride of thine heart, O thou that dwellest in the clefts of the rock, that holdest the height of the hill: though thou shouldest make thy nest as high as the **eagle**, I will bring thee down from thence, saith the LORD.

15. **Jeremiah 49:5.22** Behold, he shall come up and fly as the **eagle**, and spread his wings over Bozrah: and at that day shall the heart of the mighty men of Edom be as the heart of a woman in her pangs.

16. **Ezekiel 1:10** As for the likeness of their faces, they four had the face of a man, and the face of a lion, on the right side: and they four had the face of an ox on the left side; they four also had the face of an **eagle**.

17. **Ezekiel 10:14** And every one had four faces: the first face was the face of a cherub, and the second face was the face of a man, and the third the face of a lion, and the fourth the face of an **eagle**.

18. **Ezekiel 17:3** Say to them, This is what the sovereign Lord says: A great **eagle** with powerful wings, long feathers and full plumage of varied colors, came to Lebanon. Taking hold of the top cedar,

19. **Ezekiel 17:7** There was also another great **eagle** with great wings and many feathers: and, behold, this vine did bend her roots toward him, and shot forth her branches toward him, that he might water it by the furrows of her plantation.

20. **Daniel 7:4** The first was like a lion, and had **eagle's** wings: I beheld till the wings thereof were plucked, and it was lifted up from the

earth, and made stand upon the feet as a man, and a man's heart was given to it.

21. **Hosea 8:1** Set the trumpet to thy mouth. He shall come as an **eagle** against the house of the LORD, because they have transgressed my covenant, and trespassed against my law.

22. **Obadiah 1:4** Though thou exalt thyself as the **eagle**, and though thou set thy nest among the stars, thence will I bring thee down, saith the LORD.

23. **Micah 1:16** Make thee bald, and poll thee for thy delicate children; enlarge thy baldness as the **eagle**; for they are gone into captivity from thee.

24. **Habakkuk 1:8** Their horses also are swifter than the leopards, and are more fierce than the evening wolves: and their horsemen shall spread themselves, and their horsemen shall come from far; they shall fly as the **eagle** that hasteth to eat.

25. **Revelation 4:7** And the first beast was like a lion, and the second beast like a calf, and the third beast had a face as a man, and the fourth beast was like a flying **eagle.**

26. **Revelation 12:14** And to the woman were given two wings of a great **eagle**, that she might fly into the wilderness, into her place, where she is nourished for a time, and times, and half a time, from the face of the serpent.

The eagle takes great care of his mate and the young eaglets. He has time for the family. There is love and warmth in the family of eagles. The eagle is the role model to mankind.

Care is an important thing in life. People don't care how much you know, until they know how much you care!

Chapter 15

The eagle and the sun

The eagle can fly directly to the glaring sun, face unwaveringly upon it to identify with it. The Eagle also has a second eyelid that allows them to look directly into the sun **s**o the eagle doesn't have to change its direction to avoid the sun.

During sickness: The sun plays a major role in the life of an eagle and is therefore the main source of healing. Like any other creature, the eagle does at times get sick. It then finds a favourate spot in the mountain and awaits for the rays of the sun to heal it.

When an eagle dies: The eagle's death is inexplicable but a very beautiful revival for Christians. An eagle seems to have a premonition when its death approaches; it leaves its nest and fly to its favourable spot in the mountain, at the edge of the cliff. It places itself right at the rim of the precipice. It wraps its wings, The eagle places itself precisely in this situation fastening its talons on the front of the rock—***always a rock.***

Feet on a rock looking straight into the sun. The eagle stays there, facing into the rising or setting sun until it dies, at which time it tumbles down the cliff. When eagles die, they face the sun willingly, it is their choice to do so. They die in an amazingly dignified way, by facing the light rather than darkness. They die facing the Lord of Lords, King of kings. Our Lord and ultimate hope.

Christians should die looking towards Jesus as our source of hope and comfort. Never ever die with your eyes facing the opposite direction of the sun. We should not allow our fate or eternity to be decided by the accidental falling of a dice but by our Lord Jesus Christ.

Besides the sun, eagles dig their talons in the rock. The rock is everything to them.

The human race should not forget "**The Rock of Ages.**"

This is the stone which was rejected by the builders, which has become the cornerstone Acts 4:11; Psalm 118:22 AKJV . . . for they drank from that spiritual Rock that followed them; **and that Rock was Christ 1 Corinthians 10:1-4 AKJV.** Isaiah says to Israel that ***he has forgotten the God of salvation, and hast not been mindful of the rock of thy strength ,(Isa. 17:10 AKJV).*** The prophet Isaiah further proclaimed Jesus as ***a stone of stumbling and for a rock ofn offense to both the houses of Israel (Isa. 8:14 AKJV).***

King David praises the Lord as being his rock and fortress. He says, ***The LORD is my rock, and my fortress, and my deliverer; The God of my rock; in him will I trust: he is my shield, and the horn of my salvation, my high tower, and my refuge, my saviour; thou savest me from violence" (II Sam. 22:1-3AKJV).*** David continued his song of praise; "***For who is God, save the LORD? and who is a rock, save our God?" and "The LORD liveth; and blessed be my rock; and exalted be the God of the rock of my salvation." (2 Samuel 22:32, 47 AKJV). "The Rock of Israel spake to me, He that ruleth over men must be just, ruling in the fear of God" (2 Samuel 23:3 AKJV).***

We must place our total confidence in the Rock of Israel for our salvation we can therefore say; Truly my soul waiteth upon God: from him cometh my salvation. He only is my rock and my salvation; he is my defence ; I shall not be greatly moved" ***(Psalm 62:1-2 AKJV).***

In ***2 Samuel 22:2*** the psalmist says ***The Lord is my rock, my fortress and my deliverer.*** In Psalm 61:2 he calls Him the rock that is higher than I.

Yes Jesus Christ, The Rock Of Ages, is there as our safe refuge, our rock of safety, our rock of assurance.

Jesus Christ is the rock upon which the church is founded, the rock out of whom rivers of living waters flow, the rock that begat Israel, Christ was and is Israel's rock of strength and protection. I cannot overemphasize the significance of This Rock in the lives of Christians. The eagle-minded Christian needs to stick to this rock for his survival and livelihood. The church of God must be Christ—centred and not denomination—centred.

The spirit of denominationalism has driven this Rock of Ages out of our church services. Man—made church Constitutions dominate the spirit of our churches. The Holy Spirit has no place in the lives of many spiritual leaders. The Bible has been replaced by manuals and constitutions which are used by church leaders to indoctrinate their members. These constitutions which are often not in line with the word of God, lead people into believing that obeying them will lead them to heaven. Minor differences cause a division in the church of God. It seems man, the crown of the creation of God has lost direction. Man does not know what he wants. Forgiveness is foreign to many of us. We need the Rock of our salvation, the Rock of ages more than anything else in all the areas of our daily activities. It is God 's intention that man must fall on this rock for deliverance.

We shall not fail, we will not fail we dare not to fail in our daily endeavours to achieve success.

www.ingramcontent.com/pod-product-compliance
Ingram Content Group UK Ltd.
Pitfield, Milton Keynes, MK11 3LW, UK
UKHW041916190726
13854UKWH00003B/1271